BUILDING THE
PANAMA CANAL

BUILDING THE
PANAMA CANAL
BY SUE VANDER HOOK

Content Consultant
Richard D. Morgan
Former General Services Director
Panama Canal Commission

ABDO
Publishing Company

CREDITS

Published by ABDO Publishing Company, 8000 West 78th Street, Edina, Minnesota 55439. Copyright © 2010 by Abdo Consulting Group, Inc. International copyrights reserved in all countries. No part of this book may be reproduced in any form without written permission from the publisher. The Essential Library™ is a trademark and logo of ABDO Publishing Company.

Printed in the United States of America,
North Mankato, Minnesota
092009
012010

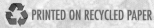 PRINTED ON RECYCLED PAPER

Editor: Jessica Hillstrom
Copy Editor: Paula Lewis
Interior Design and Production: Rebecca Daum
Cover Design: Rebecca Daum

Library of Congress Cataloging-in-Publication Data
Vander Hook, Sue, 1949-
  Building the Panama Canal / Sue Vander Hook.
     p. cm. — (Essential events)
  Includes bibliographical references and index.
  ISBN 978-1-60453-942-4
  1. Panama Canal (Panama)—History—Juvenile literature. 2.
Canals—Panama—Design and construction—History—Juvenile
literature. 3. Canal Zone—History—Juvenile literature. I. Title.
  F1569.C2V36 2010
  972.87′5—dc22

                            2009030373

TABLE OF CONTENTS

Giant excavators helped "make the dirt fly" at the bottom of the Panama Canal.

"MAKE THE DIRT FLY!"

President Theodore "Teddy" Roosevelt's voice was loud and excited. "Make the dirt fly!" he barked at John Findley Wallace, chief engineer of the Panama Canal project.[1] Roosevelt's order was clear and his determination evident. The waterway between the Atlantic and Pacific oceans must be finished.

Building a canal across the narrow Isthmus of Panama was important to the president and the United States. It was also important to the world. For nearly 400 years, explorers and engineers from Spain, Italy, Scotland, France, and other countries had dreamed of a shortcut across Central America. Ships no longer would have to travel around Cape Horn at the southernmost tip of South America. This would decrease the travel time of their journeys by five or six months. The passageway would slash 7,000 miles (11,265 km) off voyages between New York and California alone.

Wallace had been appointed chief of the canal project on May 6, 1904. By the end of June, he was in Panama, under extreme pressure to finish what the French had begun. The Panama Canal would prove to be one of the most difficult engineering feats of all time. But Wallace's biggest obstacle during his one-year stint was

What Is an Isthmus?

An isthmus is a narrow strip of land with water on two sides that connects two larger land masses. The world's most famous isthmuses are the Isthmus of Panama and the Isthmus of Suez. In the nineteenth century, isthmuses were obstacles to sea voyages, the primary mode of long-distance travel at the time.

not how to build the canal or remove thousands of tons of dirt. His greatest challenge was the relentless, tiny mosquito.

Dr. William Gorgas

Dr. William Gorgas's first efforts to eliminate malaria and yellow fever began in Cuba. From 1896 to 1901, deaths from yellow fever in Havana, Cuba, were reduced from 1,300 to fewer than 20.

In 1903, The United States government promoted Gorgas to the rank of colonel and appointed him assistant surgeon general. The following year, Gorgas was in Panama, fighting the same diseases. His similar success in Panama eventually earned him the position of president of the American Medical Association and surgeon general of the U.S. Army.

During World War I (1914–1918), Gorgas expanded the Army Medical Corps from several hundred officers to more than 30,000 men.

TINY MOSQUITOES BECOME A BIG PROBLEM

Mosquito-borne diseases had taken the lives of tens of thousands of workers who had tried to dig the canal for France. Wallace had to find a way protect his crew from the deadly diseases. He began work immediately, as did the project's doctor, Dr. William Gorgas, and his team of physicians. Gorgas's job was to rid the construction site of yellow fever and malaria. Recently, he had been a part of a team that had nearly eradicated the two diseases in Havana, Cuba, and now he was sure he could do it in Panama.

In Cuba, Gorgas had worked with Dr. Walter Reed, a U.S. Army doctor who confirmed through experiments that yellow fever was

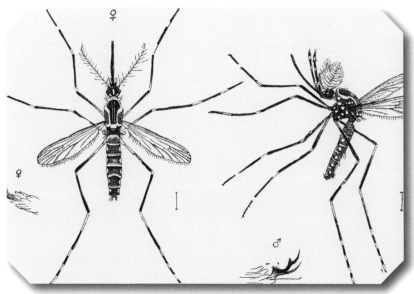

The yellow fever mosquito

transmitted by mosquitoes. But the mosquito theory was not popular among officials of the canal project. The governor of the area scolded Gorgas, "On the mosquito you are simply wild. All who agree with you are wild. Get the idea out of your head. Yellow fever, as we all know, is caused by filth."[2]

Even Wallace refused to believe that mosquitoes were to blame for disease. He proclaimed that "clean, healthy, moral Americans"[3] would not catch yellow fever. But President Roosevelt believed in Gorgas. The president gave him and his team top priority and full authority to do their jobs. Despite the critics, Gorgas began his enormous task. He set out to rid the area of two types of mosquitoes: the *Aedes aegypti*, the transmitter of yellow fever, and the *Anopheles*, the hardy carrier of malaria.

Cleaning Up Panama City

First, Gorgas ordered Panama City to be fumigated. A huge cleanup crew went from building to building and house to house. They were authorized to get rid of standing water, as that is where mosquitoes lay eggs. They were also to spray everything with insecticide. *Aedes aegypti* larvae were everywhere—in water vessels and in puddles that accumulated in people's yards.

In July, a crew visited the home of Claude Mallet, the British consul to Panama. They swept his rooms and removed anything in his yard that might hold water. They covered barrels of drinking water with wire netting and instructed Mallet to pour a layer of oil on the surface to deter mosquitoes. After the crew left, Mallet wrote to his wife that he could now read "without having to wipe the mosquitoes off every second."[4] He proclaimed himself "a convert to the mosquito theory."[5]

A mosquito exterminator

Despite the cleanup, a severe epidemic of yellow fever broke out. Gorgas ordered another sweep of the city. But the disease spread again—and Gorgas's opponents adopted an I-told-you-so attitude. But Gorgas did not give up. He ordered a third sweep, and this time it was successful. Large outbreaks of yellow fever ceased, and by 1906, the disease had practically vanished from the canal site.

It would take longer, however, to control the *Anopheles*, the malaria-carrying mosquito. Once again, Gorgas was not deterred by the enormity of his task. He organized 1,200 men into 25 districts along the 50-mile (80-km) construction site. Over the next ten years, his team repeatedly cleared away mosquitoes from sections of a narrow strip on either side of the canal. They drained swamps, destroyed weeds that grew in water, and spread insecticide and chloroform wherever they went. They also used a mixture of carbolic acid, resin, and caustic soda. These made up a powerful weapon against mosquitoes. Sometimes, Gorgas's men resorted to smacking mosquitoes with flyswatters or their hands. And Gorgas's team made sure workers slept under mosquito nets and had screens on their windows.

Canal personnel lived in constant fear that they would come down with a deadly disease. Although they were encouraged to bring family members to Panama, most people turned down the offer. John Barrett,

What Is Yellow Fever?

Yellow fever is also called black vomit, yellow jack, or American Plague. It is transmitted to humans by mosquitoes, which, in turn, were infected by monkeys or humans with the disease. Three to six days after being bitten by an infected mosquito, a person experiences fever, chills, headache, muscle aches, vomiting, and backache. As the disease progresses, it leads to internal bleeding as well as kidney and liver failure. When the liver fails, the skin and whites of the eyes turn yellow, the reason for the name "yellow fever." The virus exists mainly in South America and Africa.

U.S. foreign minister to Panama, had planned to bring his mother there. But at the height of a yellow fever epidemic in December 1904, he changed his mind. "If you should be unwell here," he wrote to her, "or if anything should happen to you I could never forgive myself for bringing you to Panama."[6]

Wallace, however, brought his wife with him as an example to his workers. He also had two metal coffins shipped over—just in case. Wallace's secretary, John Seager, also sent for his wife. They

A Lot of Cleaning Supplies

In order for Dr. Gorgas to wage his campaign against mosquitoes, he needed supplies. He spent $90,000 on wire screening alone. Each month, he ordered 120 tons (109 tonnes) of pyrethrum powder, 300 tons (272 tonnes) of sulfur, and 50,000 gallons (189,271 L) of kerosene oil. He also had the following supplies shipped immediately:

- 3,000 garbage cans
- 4,000 buckets
- 1,000 brooms
- 500 scrub brushes
- 5,000 pounds (2,268 kg) of soap
- 1,200 fumigation pots
- 240 rat traps

His list also included carbolic acid, wood alcohol, mercurial chloride, padlocks, lanterns, machetes, and lawn mowers. Gorgas's fumigation team consisted of hundreds of men toting ladders, pots, buckets, oil, and more. They sought out mosquitoes, larvae, standing water, and people ill with yellow fever. The men also installed running water, eliminating the centuries-old practice of storing drinking water in jars, barrels, and cisterns. Other methods they used to eliminate mosquitoes included cutting grass, breeding fish that fed on the surface of water (where mosquitoes bred), and bringing in spiders, lizards, and ants that fed on mosquitoes.

Trains for the Dead

Trains called funerary trains regularly carried dead bodies out of the Culebra Cut, the center section of the canal. The trains were loaded with bodies of workers who had died on the job. The bodies were taken to Colón, where they were buried in graves marked with a small cross. One worker, S. W. Plume, recalled, "From Colón the Panama Railroad ran regular funeral trains out to Monkey Hill each morning. Over to Panama it was the same way— bury, bury, bury, running two, three, and four trains a day. . . . They died like animals."[8]

were newlyweds, married only two months. Shortly after her arrival in January 1905, Seager's new bride died abruptly from yellow fever. Her death shocked American canal employees. Panama's Governor George Davis commented on the tragedy, "Naturally this death among those that are so well known has almost caused a panic in the ranks of the American employees of the Canal Commission."[7]

In April, O. M. Johnson, one of the canal architects, came down with headaches, back pain, extreme thirst, and black vomit. He died that month of yellow fever. Johnson was buried in one of Wallace's metal coffins.

A DEADLY PROJECT

During the French and the U.S. construction of the Panama Canal, more than 27,000 workers died. Most died from disease, although others died from accidents and landslides. For some, their graveyard was the mud along the canal route. Thousands of others would be buried in a cemetery on a hill outside Colón, the seaport that would one day be the Atlantic entrance to the Panama Canal.

Despite the hazards, workers kept going with an unstoppable determination. Their efforts and resolve paid off. In August 1914, ten years after the United States began the project, the Panama Canal officially opened. The canal immediately changed the shipping industry by providing a vital route for world trade. It also became a popular shortcut for international voyages. In the twenty-first century, the canal is still extremely significant to commerce and world travel. Today, approximately 5 percent of the world's commerce passes through the waterway.

Much of the credit for the canal's success was attributed to Dr. Gorgas, whose work to eradicate disease did not go unnoticed. President Roosevelt appointed him to the Panama Canal Commission. A fellow doctor praised his accomplishment: "There is nothing to match the work of Gorgas in the history of human achievement."[9] But Gorgas gave the credit to Dr. Ronald Ross, who first discovered the malaria parasite. In a 1914 letter to Ross, Gorgas wrote,

"It seems to me not extreme, therefore, to say that it was your discovery of this fact that has enabled us to build the canal at the Isthmus of Panama."[10]

Early explorers were on the right track when they sought a pathway between the Atlantic and Pacific oceans. Although they never saw the Panama Canal, they deserve credit for creating the dream. It was a dream that began in the early sixteenth century when explorers and conquistadors from Europe first sailed the Atlantic along the coast of Central America. They explored mountains, rivers, and swamps in search of gold. They sailed on the Atlantic Ocean and heard about "the other sea" where a kingdom overflowed with gold. They did not find a kingdom of gold, but they did find another sea—across the isthmus that one day would become the site of the Panama Canal.

Dr. William Gorgas

Panamanian guides showed Balboa the Pacific Ocean in 1513.

A Path Between the Seas

hristopher Columbus was the first European known to visit Panama. His fleet of four ships left Spain in May 1502. The voyage was Columbus's fourth journey funded by Queen Isabella. Nearly three months later, the ships arrived at Central America off the coast of what is now Honduras. For several months, Columbus sailed along the coastline exploring present-day Honduras, Nicaragua, and Costa Rica. He was looking for a hidden passageway to the East, a waterway through the narrow land.

On October 16, 1502, Columbus arrived at the land known today as Panama, where natives told him of a channel of water that led to gold and another sea. Columbus and his men followed the natives up the Chagres River and into the dense jungles. But instead of finding a kingdom of gold and a sea, they became stranded in shallow water. The men were forced to abandon their expedition.

That did not stop other explorers from looking for a passageway to the East. Eleven years later, in 1513, Spanish conquistador Vasco Núñez de Balboa, along with 190 other Spaniards and several bloodhounds, set out on foot through Panama's Darién Jungle. They trekked through thick vines, climbed mountains, and crossed rivers on makeshift tree-trunk bridges. Along the way, one-third of the men died, either from heatstroke, disease, or hostile natives.

THE OCEAN IN VIEW

But Balboa did not give up. On September 25, 1513, his Panamanian guides showed him a spot where he could see the other ocean. Balboa climbed to the top of a hill and looked out on a huge body of water—the Pacific Ocean. After kneeling in prayer, he called for his men. He wanted to show them "the great maine sea heretofore vnknowne [unknown] to the inhabitants of Europe, Aphrike [Africa], and Asia."[1]

Balboa sent word back to the king of Spain and recommended that Spain continue searching for a waterway between the two oceans. In his message, Balboa included an interesting suggestion from one of his engineers: If a waterway is not found, "it might not be impossible to make one."[2] Thus was born the idea of a human-made canal across the Isthmus of Panama.

Financed by powerful kings and queens, explorers continued to search for a water route to the Pacific Ocean. From 1519 to 1521, Portuguese explorer Ferdinand

Climbing the Mountains

In order to travel north or south through Panama, one had to cross the steep, rocky terrain of the Tabasará Mountains. These mountains stretch almost the entire length of Panama. They tower an average of 5,000 feet (1,500 m) above sea level. Large rivers, such as the Chagres, flow abundantly through the Tabasará Mountains.

Magellan reached the Pacific Ocean a different way. He endured a long, perilous journey around Cape Horn at the southern tip of South America. But the voyage was so long and hazardous that others grew even more determined to find a route across Central America.

By 1530, no waterway connecting the oceans had been found. The realization that there was no hidden river across the isthmus sparked again the idea of a human-made waterway. In 1534, King Charles V of Spain ordered the Chagres River in Panama cleared as far as possible. Then he wanted the land surveyed to choose the ideal path for a canal. But the dream of building a canal did not come true during Charles's reign. A water passage would not be built for nearly 400 years. In the meantime, a footpath—called the *Camino Real,* which translates to the Royal Road—served as the main overland route. Along the path, gold, silver, and other precious cargo flowed in a constant stream from the Americas to Europe.

Traders used the Royal Road for many years, but the dream of a waterway stayed alive. It was obvious that ships could carry more goods more quickly than men and mules trudging through the jungle for weeks at a time. But ideas and plans for a canal failed again and again. In the 1730s, the French devised at least four plans for a waterway, but political pressures continually impeded progress. It would be a new political power—the newly formed United States of America—that would boost worldwide interest in a canal across Central America.

Even before the American colonists won their independence, Benjamin Franklin, their representative to France, was advocating canals. He pushed for canals to be built across Panama as well as across the isthmus on the eastern border of Egypt. Thomas Jefferson, the next ambassador to France and later the third president of the United States, was also fascinated with the idea. "With respect to the Isthmus of Panama," he wrote

The Canal Age

The first half of the nineteenth century is sometimes referred to as the "canal age." The Caledonian Canal opened in Scotland in 1822, joining the North Sea and the Atlantic Ocean. In 1825, the Erie Canal opened, connecting the Hudson River and the Great Lakes in North America. Then a nearly 100-mile (161-km) route called the Illinois and Michigan Canal was dug in 1848 between Chicago and LaSalle, connecting the Great Lakes and the Mississippi River. Clearly an increasingly industrialized world demanded better and quicker passages for boats and ships. Early U.S. leaders such as George Washington and Benjamin Franklin had believed that canals were the key to the future of the New World.

in a letter, "I am assured . . . that a canal appeared very practicable."[3]

Other U.S. presidents became interested. President Andrew Jackson was the first to send a team to Panama to scope out a site. In 1835, a group of U.S. Army engineers visited the country to determine what it would take to build a canal. After just a few days, they proclaimed that Panama's topography was too rugged. It would be nearly impossible, they claimed, to build a canal across the isthmus.

The United States was not the only country investigating a water route through Central America. Surveyors and engineers from France, Great Britain, Italy, Denmark, Holland, and other nations converged on the narrowest parts of the isthmus to find the perfect spot to construct a waterway. Nicaragua and Panama were the top site choices. The race was on for who would be the first to come up with a workable plan.

The Scottish in Panama

In the 1690s, Scotland attempted to establish a colony on the Isthmus of Panama. In November 1698, five ships carrying 1,200 Scotsmen sailed to the Bay of Caledonia in Panama. But New Caledonia, as it was called, soon turned into a disaster. Within six months, disease, insects, starvation, and sweltering heat had taken its toll on the settlers. More than 70 percent of the New Caledonians died. They abandoned the project after seven months.

THE RUSH FOR GOLD

In 1846, the demand for a canal increased. The U.S. acquisition of California and the Oregon Territory heightened the urgency to find a better way to travel from America's East Coast to the West Coast. In 1849, the discovery of gold in California sent the world into a frenzy. Thousands of gold prospectors from all over the world could not get to California quickly enough. Loaded down with picks, shovels, and pans, they looked for the fastest route to this western state where they hoped to find their fortune.

At the time, there were three routes that Americans could take to California. They could travel across the United States on horseback or by covered wagon. These were the slowest modes. They could go by ship from New York City around the southern tip of South America and up to California. But this was a very long trip. Or they could go by ship to Panama, take a boat up the Chagres River, and then walk to the

What Is the Continental Divide?

Travelers crossing over the mountains in Panama in the 1850s were actually crossing the Continental Divide. The Continental Divide is a natural dividing line that runs through North America. The divide separates water that flows in two directions. In the Tabasará Mountains in Panama, rivers on the north side flow into the Atlantic Ocean, while those originating on the south side flow into the Pacific. The Continental Divide begins in Alaska and runs 8,000 miles (12,870 km) south to the Panama Canal.

Pacific Ocean. The walk, however, was treacherous. Travelers had to trudge through thick jungles and over the rocky hills of the Continental Divide. One American said the trip was "so like a nightmare that one took it as a bad dream—in helpless silence."[4] Once they reached the Pacific Ocean, travelers waited for the occasional arrival of a ship on its way to California. Sometimes thousands of Americans were stranded on the coast, waiting for passage to the Golden State. Crude camps were set up, but diseases ran rampant in these crowded, dirty living quarters and hundreds died. The Panama route was the quickest, but it was also the most treacherous.

An 1850 Travel Guide

During the California Gold Rush (1848–1855), prospectors and fortune seekers searched frantically for the fastest route to California. In 1850, *Gregory's Guide for California Travelers via the Isthmus of Panama* encouraged prospectors to come ashore at Panama and cross on land: "The voyage [to California] by way of Cape Horn will occupy on an average, five or six months, while by the Isthmus route, the trip is accomplished in as many weeks!"[5]

If Not by Boat, Then by Rail

William Aspinwall, an American businessman, ran a steamship company that offered passage between New York and Panama. With the Gold Rush in high gear, he seized the opportunity to build a railroad across the isthmus. Construction began on the Panama Railroad in May 1850. However, workers soon realized that building a railway through swamps swarming with mosquitoes and rampant with wild animals would not be an easy task. Workers died in droves, but construction went on. More railroad track was added each year. In the meantime, eager gold diggers rode by train as far as they could and then walked the rest of the way.

In 1852, a notable passenger rode on Aspinwall's railroad. He was Lieutenant Ulysses S. Grant, who would become president of the United States in 1869. With him were soldiers of the Fourth Infantry and their families. On the way across Panama, cholera struck, and more than 100 people in Grant's party died. Grant did not forget his eventful trip. As president, he sent out seven expeditions to study the possibility of building a canal somewhere across Central America.

Trade and travel over the next 25 years increased dramatically in the United States. The demand for a fast, safe route across Central America was growing. But it would be the French who would begin the daunting task of constructing a waterway across Panama.

Gold seekers crossed the Isthmus of Panama on their way to California in the 1850s.

Ferdinand de Lesseps

THE FRENCH BEGIN THE DIG

The United States was not happy that France was going to build a canal through Panama. Ulysses S. Grant, who became president in 1869, had worked diligently with his canal commission to choose the best site for a waterway. The commission had chosen Nicaragua. Then in May 1879, U.S. newspapers published news of France's plan. The French were depending on one man—Ferdinand de Lesseps—to accomplish the enormous task. Lesseps was not an engineer or architect, but he was known as a man who could get things done.

THE DREAM GETS WINGS

Lesseps had already earned worldwide fame for successfully building the extraordinary Suez Canal through Egypt. The 119-mile (192-km) canal, which had been open for ten years, linked the Mediterranean Sea and the Red Sea. Ships no longer had to navigate around Africa, and goods no longer had to be carried on foot across the Isthmus of Suez. The Suez Canal had significantly changed world trade, and ships were traveling around the world in record time.

A charming, intelligent developer, Lesseps was the world's logical choice to head up a canal project in Panama. He also had the approval of the International Congress for the Study of an Interoceanic Canal, a

The First Transcontinental Railroad

In 1869, the same year Lesseps finished construction of the Suez Canal, the United States completed the First Transcontinental Railroad—referred to as the Iron Horse. The railroad linked the East and West coasts of the United States. It also revolutionized American travel and helped businesses by carrying cargo quickly and cheaply.

prestigious body of representatives from 22 nations. Lesseps planned to construct the canal by digging down to sea level—as was done in the Suez Canal. But Lesseps did not realize the folly of his plan. The terrain in Panama was much different from the flat, sandy desert of Egypt. In Egypt, the project was to build a ditch through a desert. But in Panama, a huge mountain range snaked through the country. To complicate matters, the Atlantic and Pacific coasts were not at the same level. The Chagres River also zigzagged through the isthmus, creating its own set of problems. But Lesseps insisted he could build a tunnel under the raging waters. He was willing to stake his reputation on his design. "I maintain," Lesseps claimed, "that Panama will be easier to make,

The Suez Canal

The Suez Canal in Egypt opened on November 17, 1869, after nearly 11 years of construction. The single-lane canal is 118 miles (190 km) long, with four places where ships can pass. It is operated by the Suez Canal Authority of the Arab Republic of Egypt. The canal has no locks because the terrain is flat. Also, there is little difference in sea level between the Mediterranean Sea at one end and the Gulf of Suez at the other. Ships sail the length of the canal in 12 to 15 hours. They travel at slow speeds of about 8 knots (9.3 mph) to prevent wakes that might erode the banks of the canal. About 7.5 percent of the world's sea trade passes through the Suez Canal. In 2007, approximately 18,000 vessels traveled the canal. Every ship must pay a toll. In 2007, ships paid an average cost of $150,000.

easier to complete, and easier to keep up
than Suez."[1]

THE DIG BEGINS

A year later, in January 1881, Lesseps's crew
ceremoniously set off a blast at Culebra, the
mountain range that would prove to be one of
Lesseps's greatest obstacles. Work officially began on
February 1, and workers started blasting rock and
removing dirt.

That year, Lesseps's company bought the rights
to the Panama Railroad. Lesseps had chosen the
railroad's route for the canal. And workers began
arriving from all over the world—the Caribbean
Islands, Europe, and the United States.

Most of the workers, however, did not realize that
the jungles teemed with pumas and jaguars and some
of the world's deadliest snakes. At night, workers
were attacked by spiders, ants, ticks, chiggers, flies,
mosquitoes, and myriad other insects that crawled
or stung. From April to December, torrents of
rain gushed from the sky almost daily. Sometimes
6 inches (15 cm) fell in one day. The Chagres River
often flooded, causing mud slides and turning the
dirt into a sticky goo.

The flat desert terrain of the Suez Canal during construction in 1869

The cities were just as dangerous. One reporter described Colón on the Atlantic Coast:

> There are neither sewers nor street cleaners . . . toilets are quite unknown, all the rubbish is thrown into the swamps or onto rubbish heaps. Toads splash in the liquid muck . . . rats infest the solid filth . . . snakes hunt both toads and rats; clouds of mosquitoes swarm into the homes.[2]

But the work went on, and workers adapted. Approximately 2,000 people now lived and worked at the site. Simple houses and barracks were erected for them nearby. Huge machinery arrived by ship, but the hodgepodge of steam shovels, trucks, locomotives, and more did not always fit the equipment already at the site. The array of machines was not always as impressive as it appeared.

SICKNESS AND EARTHQUAKE SLOW PROGRESS

The Grand Hotel in Panama City was turned into headquarters. First-rate hospitals were erected to care for the sick. In the summer of 1881, at the height of the rainy season, yellow fever hit with a vengeance. Approximately 400 people died by 1882. Since no one was sure how yellow fever or malaria spread, it was impossible to take precautions. A French engineer wrote:

> *These successive deaths . . . had shaken our courage, striking the imaginations of even the bravest men; everyone anxiously began thinking of steamers home; in a word, we were struck by one of those moral weaknesses from which a panic is born.*[3]

The Country of Panama

Panama stretches more than 500 miles (800 km). It connects Costa Rica in Central America on the west to Columbia in South America in the east. Panama boasts more than 1,500 miles (2,400 km) of coastline and has a population of more than 3.3 million people. Its primary language is Spanish, although many people also speak English.

The White Man's Graveyard

During the building of the Panama Canal by the French, approximately one in five French workers died of disease. Because people believed that more whites died of tropical diseases than blacks, the Canal Zone was dubbed "the white man's graveyard."

Lesseps downplayed the deaths so new workers would not be afraid to come to Panama. His attitude earned him the nickname "the Great Undertaker." (An undertaker is someone who handles the dead.) A cartoon caption in *Harper's Weekly* read, "Is M. de Lesseps a Canal Digger or a Grave Digger?"[4]

By 1882, some people were beginning to wonder about Lesseps's ability to handle the enormous job ahead of him. At the age of 77, he was less often at the work site. His son Charles increasingly took on more leadership duties. On a tour of Panama, Charles found that nature had not been kind to the men or the equipment. Rust had assaulted anything made of iron or steel, and mold grew on clothes, shoes, books, and other items. Then an earthquake shook the isthmus on September 7. It was unlike any the area had experienced in recorded history. Buildings collapsed, railroad tracks crumbled, and roads sunk. The earth opened up in the city of Colón, leaving a crack 400 feet (122 m) long down one of the streets.

THE FRENCH PROJECT FAILS

The construction site experienced its share of damage, which made an already unbearable situation worse. But no earthquake or other natural disaster ultimately caused the French project to fail. The failure was due to a series of wrong choices—the wrong type of canal, the wrong route, the wrong equipment. In the end, bankruptcy caused the French to abandon the project ten years after it had begun.

Lesseps's most fatal error in building the canal was his construction plan. He had attempted to excavate the entire 50-mile (80-km) stretch down to sea level. The Atlantic coast was at sea level, but the Pacific coast was much higher. In between was a variety of levels, including the mountains that ran along the Continental Divide. Locks would have been the best solution because they would allow ships to be raised up and down to match the various levels of the canal. But Lesseps argued that dynamite could blow a deep enough slice through the mountains. This would allow for digging deep trenches. Then the waters from both oceans would seep into the canal and fill it up. Lesseps thought locks were unnecessary.

Lesseps's choice of a route was also flawed. He had chosen the route along the railroad because it was the shortest distance across the isthmus. It also provided an easy way to haul away thousands of tons of dirt by rail. But the Chagres River often flooded the tracks. At other places, the railroad ascended to the tops of the highest mountains.

Eventually, Lesseps was defeated by the overwhelming task. He finally admitted that a multilevel lock canal should have been built. But it was too late. Lesseps retired in France in 1889. He faced charges of mismanagement of funds and fraud. His status changed from hero to cheater and liar. Lesseps confided to his wife, "What a terrible nightmare I have had."[5] He died five years later at the age of 89.

The French were gone, but they left behind a burning question: who would take over where they had left off?

Premature explosion in the building of the Panama Canal in the 1900s

U.S. politicians disagreed over where in Central America to build a canal. At first, most politicians favored Nicaragua over Panama.

Nicaragua or Panama?

fter France's failed attempt to build a waterway across Central America, the United States was still considering the possibility. In the 1890s and early 1900s, the U.S. economy was growing rapidly, and its navy was expanding.

A canal would boost international trade and improve the navy's mobility. But Nicaragua—not Panama—was the U.S. government's preferred site.

Senator John Tyler Morgan of Alabama was a vocal advocate for a canal. He believed it was important for the United States to control the waterway. He also was sure the canal had to run through Nicaragua. Enthusiasm among Congress members was high. It looked as though they would approve it. But then two individuals—William Nelson Cromwell and Philippe Bunau-Varilla—began lobbying Congress for a canal in Panama.

Lobbying for Panama

Cromwell, a fast-talking New York attorney, had a reputation for fixing troubled corporations and arranging enormous mergers. One of his clients was the New Panama Canal Company, which was Lesseps's company reorganized under a new name. Cromwell's goal was to convince the United States to buy the French company that had failed to build a canal across Panama. He set out to persuade the politicians in Washington DC to change their minds. He had to turn them away from Nicaragua and point them directly at Panama.

Bunau-Varilla had worked with Lesseps in Panama as engineer-in-chief of the canal project. He had invested more than $400,000 of his own money in the project, and he intended to recover his losses. Now he started his U.S. crusade, a task, he said, that "seemed impossible of achievement!"[1]

He gave his first speech on January 16, 1901, to a group of businessmen in Cincinnati, Ohio. He trumpeted the advantages of a canal in Panama. He said the route was shorter and straighter, would require fewer locks, and would cost less to run. Panama had better harbors, he claimed, and a railroad was already in place. The first attempt to build the Panama Canal had not failed because of technical difficulties, he told them, but because of financial problems. He did not mention the floods, the mud slides, the yellow fever, or the malaria. And he downplayed the mountains, the rainfall, the winds, the lakes, and the raging Chagres River, which he called "this monster of the imagination."[2]

Most importantly, Bunau-Varilla reminded his listeners that Panama had no volcanoes. And then he told about the numerous volcanoes in Nicaragua and the 1835 eruption of the Coseguina that had lasted almost two days. He also mentioned the active volcano in the center of Lake Nicaragua. Ometepe (now called Concepción) had erupted in 1880 after a long quiet period. It had erupted again in 1883 and 1889.

Bunau-Varilla continued to paint a dreary picture of Nicaragua, where, he said, canals would fill with ash from erupting volcanoes. His audience was fascinated. He eventually took his argument all the way to President William McKinley at the White House. He also made his way to the home of his strongest opponent, John Tyler Morgan. This chief advocate of a Nicaragua canal did not hesitate to argue with Bunau-Varilla and expose his motives. Standing face-to-face with his adversary, Morgan thundered, "Now, between ourselves, you would not put one dollar of your own money in this absurd project—in this rotten project—of Panama!"[3] Bunau-Varilla left hastily. On April 11, 1901, he boarded a ship to France.

In September, President William McKinley was assassinated and Vice President Theodore Roosevelt

Volcano Momotombo

Momotombo is a volcano on the shores of Managua, the capital of Nicaragua. It has become somewhat of a symbol for Nicaragua. Images of the volcano appear on postage stamps, murals, and matchboxes. An eruption in 1610 forced the people of a nearby Spanish settlement to evacuate. Momotombo erupted again in 1905—just three years after the U.S. Congress rejected a site in the vicinity for a canal.

became president. A canal in Central America became one of Roosevelt's top priorities. He believed it was important for U.S. battleships to have a quick, direct sea route in case war broke out. As past assistant secretary of the U.S. Navy, he had firsthand experience with war. He had fought in Cuba during the Spanish-American War in 1898. The United States was helping this small island in the Atlantic Ocean fight for its independence from Spain.

Spain was accused of blowing up the USS *Maine* battleship in Cuba's Havana Harbor on February 15, 1898. Roosevelt ordered the USS *Oregon* to Cuba. On March 19, the ship set sail from San Francisco and headed around the southern tip of South America. Americans became wrapped up in the perilous 12,000-mile (19,312-km) journey of one of the country's largest battleships. Weeks went by where the navy lost communication with the ship. But finally, after a 67-day voyage, the *Oregon* arrived in Cuba, just in time to participate in the Battle of Santiago Bay. Americans cheered the timely arrival of the *Oregon*, but they also championed the cause of a Central American canal. If there had been a canal, the *Oregon*'s voyage would have been only 4,000 miles (6,437 km)—one-third the distance.

A canal became even more urgent to Roosevelt. In a December 3, 1901, speech to Congress, Roosevelt, now president, declared, "No single great material work which remains to be undertaken on this continent is of such consequence to the American people."[4]

CONGRESS VOTES

In June 1902, the canal vote finally came before Congress. Three days before the vote, Cromwell had sent a ten-cent Nicaraguan postage stamp to every member of Congress. On the stamp was a picture of the Momotombo volcano erupting. Although Momotombo had been dormant

One of the Greatest Presidents

Vice President Theodore Roosevelt became president of the United States on September 14, 1901. His predecessor, President William McKinley, died from a bullet wound inflicted eight days earlier by his assassin, Leon Frank Czolgosz. The 42-year-old Roosevelt became the youngest person to ever hold the office of president. In 1904, he was elected president in his own right and served until 1909. Roosevelt was enthusiastic about building a canal across the Isthmus of Panama. Later he would consider it his most significant international achievement. During his presidency, Roosevelt greatly increased the size of the U.S. Navy to demonstrate a growing American military might. He established the Great White Fleet—16 extraordinary battleships with white hulls and red, white, and blue banners on their bows. The fleet toured the world from 1907 to 1909.

Roosevelt was awarded the Nobel Peace Prize in 1906 for negotiating peace in the Russo-Japanese War. He was loved by the masses and is consistently rated by historians as one of the greatest U.S. presidents of all time.

A Nicaragua Canal

The idea for a canal across Nicaragua did not die with the 1902 vote in favor of a Panama Canal. In 2004, Nicaragua proposed a canal that would handle ships larger than those the Panama Canal can currently handle. The Nicaragua proposal would accommodate ships up to 250,000 tons (226,800 tonnes). Ships up to 65,000 tons (58,970 tonnes) can presently fit through the locks at the Panama Canal.

for years and was 100 miles (161 km) from the proposed canal site, the stamp cast doubt on Nicaragua. Cromwell made sure a story about the volcano appeared in the *New York Sun* as well.

On June 19, 1902, Congress voted in favor of a canal in Panama. On June 28, Congress passed the Spooner Act, approving $40 million to purchase France's rights to a canal in Panama. Bunau-Varilla would get his investment back, and Roosevelt would have boasting rights for the most significant event of his presidency. "I took Panama. . . I built the canal" he would say again and again.[5]

The United States now owned the right to build the Panama Canal. However, it would have one more major political hurdle—Colombia—before construction could begin. Colombia controlled Panama and had the power to approve or deny a canal. And Colombia disliked the United States for its role in the Spanish-American War.

President Theodore Roosevelt campaigned for election in 1904.

A 1903 cartoon showed President Theodore Roosevelt refusing to pay Colombia millions for Panama Canal rights.

ROOSEVELT AND REVOLUTION

ager to start work on the canal, President Roosevelt dispatched U.S. marines to Panama in the fall of 1902. They were there to take control of the Panama Railroad, but the Colombians had not given Americans permission to be there.

The marines eventually left, but long-term damage was done to the already shaky U.S.-Colombian relationship.

On March 17, 1903, the United States proposed the Hay-Herrán Treaty. The United States offered Colombia $10 million for a six-mile-(9.7-km-) wide strip across Panama and a yearly payment of $250,000. Colombia, however, refused to sign the treaty. Colombia demanded another $15 million. Roosevelt was infuriated, as were the Panamanians. The Panamanians wanted to negotiate a treaty directly with the United States, but the Colombian government refused. The Panamanians were not pleased, and the incident only reminded them of how long they had wanted to be an independent nation.

In October, Bunau-Varilla told Roosevelt he predicted a revolution in Panama. Surprised, Roosevelt responded, "A revolution? Would it be possible?"[1] Bunau-Varilla moved quickly. He wrote a proclamation of independence, a military plan, a constitution, and more for Panama. The U.S. Navy dispatched two

Philippe Bunau-Varilla

Philippe Bunau-Varilla (1859–1940) served in the French army during World War I and lost a leg at the Battle of Verdun. Until his death in 1940, he continued to show interest in the Panama Canal and encouraged changing it from a lock canal to a canal at sea level.

In 1911, Roosevelt admitted that he took the Panama Canal from Colombia. In 1914, Congress wanted to give Colombia $25 million and its sincere apology, but Roosevelt would not allow it. In 1921, two years after Roosevelt's death, the United States gave Colombia $25 million. In turn, Colombia recognized Panama as an independent country.

gunboats to Panama, and Roosevelt ordered the Panama Railroad to refuse transportation for Colombian troops. Then the citizens of Panama revolted.

While U.S. warships prevented Colombian soldiers from entering Panama, the Panamanians carried out a bloodless coup. They took over government buildings, and eventually the Colombians quietly went home.

Within hours, Roosevelt recognized the new Republic of Panama. On November 18, 1903, the United States and Panama agreed to the Hay-Bunau-Varilla Treaty. This treaty gave the United States a ten-mile-wide (16 km) passageway across the country, from the Atlantic Coast to the Pacific. This strip of land was called the Canal Zone.

Philippe Bunau-Varilla, acting as minister of Panama, signed the treaty, which was ratified by Panama on December 2, 1903. As a French citizen, however, he did not have authority to enter into a treaty on Panama's behalf. The United States ratified the treaty anyway on February 23, 1904. Bunau-Varilla later reflected, "I had fulfilled my mission.

I had safeguarded the work of the French genius;
I had avenged its honor; I had served France."[2]

People all over the world criticized Roosevelt
for using military force to get his way in Panama.
They called his actions "gunboat diplomacy." Riots
broke out in the streets of Bogotá, Colombia.
Representatives from Colombia set out for
Washington DC. They made desperate offers to
accept the original treaty. But Roosevelt ignored
their appeals.
Meanwhile John
Tyler Morgan
warned his fellow
senators, "I fear
that we have got too
large to be just and
the people of the
country fear it."[3] As
for Roosevelt, he
proclaimed, "I took
the Canal Zone and
left Congress to
debate."[4]

For the most
part, the American

Theodore "Teddy" Roosevelt

Before Theodore Roosevelt became president, he dabbled in political, military, and rural life. He was elected to the New York state assembly at the early age of 23 in 1881. But when Roosevelt's wife and mother both died on February 14, 1884, he went West, where he spent the next two years as a cowboy and naturalist in the Dakota Territory. However, he returned often to New York and remained in the public eye.

In 1897, President William McKinley appointed him assistant secretary of the navy, and the following year Roosevelt found himself in the middle of the Spanish-American War as leader of a group of ragtag, untrained soldiers that came to be called the "Rough Riders." Roosevelt's victories in the war brought him great popularity and landed him a victory in the race for governor of New York in 1898. In 1900, he was elected vice president to President William McKinley.

people were elated about the canal, and they adored Teddy Roosevelt. The president later stated confidently, "The one thing for which I deserved most credit in my entire administration was my action in seizing the psychological moment to get complete control of Panama."[5] He went on to say that his actions benefited Panama and the world. "The people of the United States," he said, "and the people of the Isthmus and the rest of mankind will all be the better because we dig the Panama Canal and keep order in its neighborhood."[6]

In May 1904, Roosevelt ordered construction to begin, saying, "Make the dirt fly!" Later that year, Roosevelt would easily win the next presidential election. He instructed his campaign staff to play up the Panama Canal. "We do not have a stronger card," he proclaimed.[7] He was right. The canal soon became a matter of U.S. pride and a symbol of progress. Men started signing up to go to Panama to be part of the mighty march of progress. "The French gave up . . . but we will finish!" announced a volunteer worker. Then he added, "With Teddy Roosevelt, *anything* is possible."[8]

*President Theodore Roosevelt tested a steam shovel during construction
of the Panama Canal in 1906.*

Laborers worked with excavators at the construction site in 1896. This was part of the first attempt by the French to build a canal.

JUNGLE AND CHAOS

When the Americans arrived in Panama, they found remnants everywhere of the failed French project. Fifty miles (80 km) of enormous piles of scrap lined the canal route. It was described as a "graveyard of reputations and dreams,

with the jungle, wet and wild as when Balboa first
set foot in it, reasserting its hold on the abandoned
diggings."[1]

> *All along the canal, there were: hundreds of tons of rusted*
> *and dilapidated machinery, the abandoned trains, the*
> *locomotives with trees sprouting out of their fireboxes, and*
> *great excavators wreathed in greenery, and the 2,000 ruined*
> *houses [of workers] empty except for the termites which were*
> *steadily eating them away.*[2]

Thousands of displaced workers were still in
the area. Most of them were living in poverty. They
had established homes and families in huts made
of scraps of wood and iron. And several hundred
were still working for the reorganized French canal
company. Their job was to maintain some of the
more valuable pieces of equipment and protect
French assets—just in case the United States bought
the project.

On May 6, 1904, John Findley Wallace was
appointed chief engineer of the Panama Canal
project. It was estimated that the canal would cost
$200 million, employ 50,000 men, and take ten
years to complete.

First Order of Business: Fighting Disease

Ancón Hospital

The hospital set up to care for the diseased in the Canal Zone was called Ancón Hospital. However, Gorgas's success in eradicating disease eventually led to a new name for the institution. In 1928, it became Gorgas Hospital. Congress made this change to recognize Gorgas for his notable humanitarian efforts in Panama.

Wallace arrived in Panama in June. Next to arrive was the medical team led by Dr. William Gorgas. Yellow fever and malaria had taken a high toll during the French construction. And Americans, especially Teddy Roosevelt, intended to fight and win the battle against disease. Roosevelt remembered all too vividly the U.S. troops who had died of disease in Cuba—13 times more than those who were killed by enemy fire.

Roosevelt wrote, "I feel that the sanitary and hygiene problems . . . on the Isthmus are those which are literally of the first importance, coming even before the engineering."[3] He believed that Gorgas had both the experience and skill to eradicate the deadly diseases. After all, Gorgas had stopped major epidemics in Cuba by destroying the war's tiniest but deadliest enemy—the mosquito. And Roosevelt was confident Gorgas could do it again. Not everyone was supportive of the doctor, however. They said it was "balderdash," or nonsense, that

Ancón Hospital in 1906

mosquitoes carried disease. Nevertheless, Gorgas got to work immediately, sending out hundreds of his staff to find mosquito-breeding sites.

Disappointment and Disease

Meanwhile, the engineering side of the project was plagued with discontent and confusion. Wallace described the Canal Zone as "only jungle and chaos from one end of the Isthmus to the other."[4]

The Isthmian Canal Commission, set up to oversee construction, had not yet come up with a plan. They first had to decide if the canal should be at sea level or if it should use locks. Wallace favored a sea level canal, but he did not have a plan either. While the commission was looking into suitable sites for dams and locks, engineers made improvements to the harbors at both oceans.

Many bright engineers who had arrived in the summer of 1904 were on their way home by fall. In a few short months, the disappointed workers had experienced terrible food, pitiful housing, and bad management. Their dreams of accomplishing an engineering feat had been dashed. They had hoped

What Is Malaria?

Malaria is an infectious disease. It is transmitted by the bite of an infected female mosquito. Each year, there are approximately 515 million cases of malaria around the world. Seventy percent of malaria-related deaths occur in Sub-Saharan Africa.

Malaria is characterized by cycles of high fever, chills, headache, and a burning thirst followed by a drenching sweat. Symptoms may also include fatigue, nausea, or vomiting. Quinine, a bitter powder from the bark of the cinchona tree, has long been an effective treatment for malaria. Quinine was distributed freely among French canal workers, who took it regularly with meals or wine to kill the terrible taste.

The way to prevent malaria is to keep mosquitoes away. Prevention methods include the use of repellants, insecticides, and mosquito nets. Eliminating standing water, where mosquitoes lay their eggs, is also important.

to find a way to lower the famed
Culebra Cut—the path through the
Continental Divide. The French
had dug out enough dirt and rock
to lower the passage through the
mountains from 210 feet (64 m) to
193 feet (59 m) above sea level. But the enormous
channel needed to be lowered much more.

The Snake Channel

Culebra Cut means "snake channel." *Culebra* means snake in Spanish, and *cut* is an engineering term for a channel that is dug out by humans.

One of the disheartened engineers was 22-year-
old Charles Carroll. He wrote his mother a month
after he arrived:

> I am thoroughly sick of this country and everything to do with
> the canal. . . . Everyone is afflicted with running sores. We are
> compelled to sleep in an old shed, six to a room. Rain water
> is drunk rather than the river water, because it is purer. The
> meals would sicken a dog. . . . Tell the boys at home to stay
> there, even if they get no more than a dollar a day.[5]

On November 24, 1904, the first case of yellow
fever was reported. By the end of January 1905,
yellow fever had spread to epidemic proportions.
More engineers and construction workers left
Panama, all too aware of the graves that already
dotted the country's landscape. Soon several
hundred men were leaving Panama every week.

Dr. Gorgas's wife described the mass exodus:

> The rush to get away quickly assumed the proportions of a panic. The canal force—labourers, engineers and office men alike—seemed to be possessed of one single view: "Let's get out of this hell hole," . . . and men arriving one day would take their departure the next, on the same boat if they could afford it.[6]

Among those who soon abandoned the project was John F. Wallace. After serving only one year as chief engineer, he left what he called a "godforsaken" country. He cited numerous reasons for leaving, then summed them up as "certain complications."[7]

Despite the doubt and the gloom, however, the project persevered. Some workers optimistically saw potential in the mounds of debris. Many of those new workers who came to fill the abandoned jobs proved to be more qualified. The Panama Canal would soon be on the path to success, with a new chief engineer, new workers, and a new direction.

The Yellow Fever Mosquito

The *Aedes aegypti*, or the yellow fever mosquito, thrives by living near human beings. The male feeds on fruit juices and the like. The female survives on blood, which is also necessary to mature her eggs. She prefers the blood of humans, although she can feed on any warm-blooded animal. She deposits her eggs only in water, preferably water in some sort of human-made container, such as a flower vase or barrel. Certain chemicals emitted from bacteria in the water stimulate her to lay her eggs.

Approximately 1,500 laborers arrived from the Caribbean islands on the
SS Ancon to work on the Panama Canal in 1909.

Construction at the Panama Canal in 1913

PREPARING TO DIG

On July 26, 1905, a new chief engineer, John F. Stevens, arrived in Colón. Stevens immediately took a quick tour of the Canal Zone. President Roosevelt warned Stevens that Panama was in a "devil of a mess."[1]

Roosevelt was right. Stevens saw abandoned steam shovels and derailed trains. He witnessed fearful, hungry workers looking for food in the sugarcane fields and jungles. On August 1, he stopped construction, fired unnecessary workers, and established a plan to cover four main areas: sanitation, housing and food, transportation, and equipment.

CLEANING UP PANAMA CITY

Stevens believed in the work of Dr. Gorgas. Up until now, Gorgas had been scorned and denied proper supplies. Gorgas was elated with the new leadership and immediately waged an all-out war on the mosquito.

First, Gorgas made it a punishable crime to have mosquito larvae on property. Once a week, Gorgas's team coated ponds and cisterns with oil so mosquitoes could not stay on the surface and lay their eggs. The workers searched for larvae from house to house, tacked screens over water containers, and repaired drooping gutters, which collected water.

Residents were ordered to leave their homes so the crew could fumigate. After filling in holes and cracks in the walls and doors, the team placed pans of sulfur or pyrethrum in each room. Then they sprinkled the pans with wood alcohol and set them on fire. About four hours later, they returned to remove the pans and sweep up dead mosquitoes.

Gorgas's team then began putting patients who already had yellow fever in quarantine. Mosquitoes spread the disease by feeding on blood of an infected patient and then passing it along to another person. If mosquitoes could not get to diseased patients, the spread of yellow fever would decrease. As soon as people became ill, medical personnel isolated them at Ancón Hospital. Pans of pyrethrum burned constantly in the patients' rooms.

A Natural Insect Repellent

Pyrethrum, which was used to fumigate for mosquitoes, is a natural insecticide made from the dried flowers of the chrysanthemum plant. Sometimes farmers plant chrysanthemums along-side their vegetable crops to repel insects such as aphids, ticks, and spider mites.

For 12 months, thousands of men worked ten hours a day to fight the mosquitoes. By January 1906, their efforts had paid off. Yellow fever was virtually gone from the canal site. Cases of malaria among workers also dropped from 82 percent in 1906 to less than 8 percent by 1915. Roosevelt was delighted with Gorgas's progress. And nearly every country in the world bestowed honors and awards on this doctor. Some called his the greatest achievement in public health of all time.

Housing and Feeding the Workers

Now Stevens turned to his second goal: improving housing and food. With 42,000 workers from 97 countries, the task seemed gargantuan. There were two main categories of workers. Unskilled laborers, who were paid in local silver money, were aptly named the "silver roll." They were housed in barracks with a bunk for every man. Daily inspections made sure these buildings were properly screened and the ditches were drained to ensure protection from mosquitoes. Skilled workers were dubbed the "gold roll" and paid in U.S gold currency. Housing for them was determined by their yearly salary. For every dollar, they received one square foot (.9 sq m) of living space.

Feeding all the workers was a challenge. The company under contract to supply food charged exorbitant prices, making a profit in excess of $1 million a year. Stevens cancelled the contract

Dr. William Gorgas Becomes a Knight

Dr. William Gorgas, who helped rid the Canal Zone of yellow fever and malaria, died in London in 1920. But before Gorgas died, King George V of England visited him in the hospital and knighted him for "the great work which you have done for humanity."[2]

and transferred the job to the canal
organization. Food was shipped in
and brought by rail to buildings
staffed by more than 400 workers.
Those workers made ice cream; baked
bread, cakes, and pies; and ground
and brewed coffee. By 10:00 a.m.,
nourishing food was delivered to
restaurants and mess halls along the
canal route.

Soon the Canal Zone began to
look and feel more like the United
States. In this narrow strip of land,
Americans set up residence, shopped,
dined at restaurants, and owned
businesses. Canal Zone residents
attended American-run schools and
received health care at American-run
hospitals and clinics. U.S. military
bases operated at both ends of the
canal. The Canal Zone would be
home to thousands of U.S. citizens for more than
75 years. But its formation and operation were
not without controversy and would one day lead to
considerable political tension.

Housing for the Workers

Housing improvements helped raise the morale of the canal workers and defend against disease. Houses for higher-salaried canal workers were built with cement footings. The pine floors, walls, and ceilings were either painted or stained. The roofs were made of corrugated iron. Each house had a tightly screened veranda to keep mosquito-borne disease out. Plumbing, lighting, and adequate furniture also improved living conditions.

BIG STRIDES IN TRANSPORTATION AND MACHINERY

Stevens was an expert in carrying out his third goal: better transportation. An authority on railways, Stevens had done everything from laying track to heading up one of the largest railroad companies in the United States. First, he added another track so trains could travel in both directions at the same time. He also added lines that branched out to excavation sites so dirt and debris could be transported quickly.

Entertainment for the Workers

Workers who remained in Panama for an extended period of time often became homesick and felt isolated from the world. Keeping workers busy and entertained became important to boosting morale. The U.S. government allotted $2.5 million for activities, entertainment, and recreation. Churches and Sunday schools were established, and ball fields were laid out. By the end of 1907, four Gold Roll clubs were in operation. They included bowling alleys, billiard rooms, gyms, and libraries with U.S. newspapers and magazines as well as more than 2,000 books. Organized activities were also provided. These included hikes, trail rides on horses through the jungle, boat trips, athletic competitions, sightseeing tours to the Culebra Cut or the locks, and amateur theatrical productions. Some workers joined a band, orchestra, or choir. Classes were available for Spanish, Bible study, or first aid. When visitors observed the clubs in 1908, they decided that the clubs,

fill a necessary place in the somewhat artificial life on the canal zone, where a body of loyal Americans, far removed from the uplifting influence of home and friends, are performing with genuine enthusiasm a work of great importance to their country.[3]

Canal employees enjoyed water sports at the Miraflores Locks.

The Panama Railroad had been called an engineering wonder in its day. By the winter of 1906, it was a fine-tuned 47-mile (76-km) double track through jungles, swamps, rivers, and valleys. The journey across the isthmus that had once taken five-and-a-half hours now took less than two. "I don't mind trying to make the dirt fly," Stevens declared, "now we have somewhere to put it!"[4]

At the harbors, Stevens replaced old wooden wharves with concrete piers where ships could load, unload, and refuel. He built storage buildings, installed sewers, laid water pipes, and paved roads. Finally, Stevens turned to the problem of equipment—old, broken, rusty, inadequate machinery. He established the Department of Machinery, whose task was to order equipment that would best get the job done. The department ordered 100 gigantic steam shovels for excavation, some of them big enough to chomp down on 5.5 cubic yards (4.2 m³) of dirt in one bite. Also on the list were unloaders that took soil off flat cars, spreaders that flattened out piles of soil, and track shifters that lifted up a section of track and moved it to another section. All this was in addition to locomotives, train cars, track, dredges, drills, barges, tugs, and boats.

A Lock Canal

Meanwhile, after years of heated debate and persuasive lobbying by Stevens, the U.S. Senate voted 36 to 31 in favor of a lock canal. Roosevelt signed the bill into law on June 29, 1906. By spring 1907, proper equipment was humming, railways were steaming, and workers were well fed and healthy. The United States was ready to finish the Panama Canal.

But when success was just around the corner, Stevens resigned. He had promised to stay in Panama "until success had been assured."[5] And, indeed, he had assured success. Now he returned to the United States. In a letter to Roosevelt, Stevens explained, "The reasons for my resignation were purely personal. I have never declared them, and I never will."[6]

Roosevelt determined to never again hire a chief engineer who had the freedom to quit. He handed the project over to an officer of the U.S. Army. ⌒

John F. Stevens

Pedro Miguel Locks under construction in 1910

BUILDING THE LOCKS

O n April 1, 1907, U.S. Army Corps of
Engineers Lieutenant Colonel George
Washington Goethals was appointed the third chief
engineer of the Panama Canal project. He was
one of the finest engineers in the United States,

and President Roosevelt gave him full authority over the canal. He even told members of the Isthmian Canal Commission to resign if they disagreed with Goethals.

Most of the work that remained on the canal was excavation—digging through difficult rock and soil on a scale never attempted before. Goethals stepped up the amount of dirt moved each day. He widened the bottom of the Culebra Cut from 200 to 300 feet (61 to 91 m), and he made the locks larger. He also hired more men. At one point, nearly 50,000 workers were on the job.

THE BRAIN WAGON

Goethals spent his mornings in his office. In the afternoons, he sped down the railroad in a gasoline-powered railway car, aptly dubbed the "brain wagon." He saw firsthand the progress being made in the canal's three divisions: the Atlantic Division, the Pacific Division, and the Central Division.

George Washington Goethals

George Washington Goethals never wore an army uniform while he was in charge of the Panama Canal. Someone who knew him well described him as "a tall, long-legged man with a rounded, bronzed face and snow-white hair. His moustache was also white, but stained with nicotine, for he smoked many cigarettes. . . . He wore civilian clothes with the usual awkwardness of a man who has spent most of his lifetime clothed in the uniform of his country."[1]

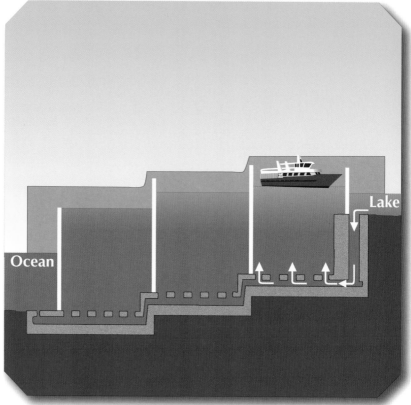

Ships entering the Panama Canal must be raised by three locks, then lowered three levels on the other side to exit the canal.

Taming the Chagres River

The Atlantic Division was the shortest section of the canal and covered 7.7 miles (12.4 km). This small section, however, had the big challenge of rerouting the Chagres River. The Chagres was unpredictable. Sometimes it was a calm trickle, but during the rainy season, it was raging and wild. It could rise as much as 20 feet (6 m) in a single day, overflowing its banks with little warning. The river crossed the canal route 14 times. Each time it flooded, work on the canal came to a standstill for several weeks.

The only way to tame the river was to build a dam. Near the town of Gatun, the river narrowed as it passed through a valley with rocky walls on either side. This made a good location for a dam. After clearing and dredging the site, workers began building the earthen dam that would eventually rise more than 100 feet (30.5 m).

When it was time to close up the dam and stop the Chagres River, the trapped water created Gatun Lake. The water supplied by this lake could be used to fill the three lock steps at varying levels. If a ship arrived from the Atlantic side, three locks would raise the ship to the higher level of Gatun Lake. When the ship arrived at the Pacific end of the canal, another three locks would lower the ship to the level of the Pacific Ocean.

The *Titanic*

When the Panama Canal locks were designed, they were to be 95 feet (29 m) wide. Goethals widened them to 110 feet (34 m) to better accommodate larger ships. One ship that could then pass through the canal would be the *Titanic*, which was under construction at that time. The *Titanic* was 92.5 feet (28.2 m) wide.

The concrete lock chambers were as long as five city blocks. Two traffic lanes were built with a total of six lock chambers each, so that ships could pass or sail in parallel from both directions.

In April 1910, trains arrived with rock that would finish damming up the powerful Chagres River. On April 22, a train dumped a load of rocks into the river. But the strength of the raging water was too much for the rocks, which catapulted downstream. William Sibert, chief engineer in the Atlantic Division, then ordered old railroad tracks to be dumped into the river. He hoped the misshapen metal would hold the rocks in place. Now the rocks and tracks both moved, slamming into a trestle, which workers scrambled

What Is a Lock?

A lock is a watertight enclosed chamber that is made of concrete, brick, or steel. It raises and lowers boats between stretches of water that are at different levels. A lock is big enough to hold the largest vessel expected to use the waterway. The position of the lock is permanent, but the water level inside varies by adding or taking out water. At both ends of the chamber are gates that seal off the chamber from the waterway. Gates open to allow a vessel to enter and close after a vessel leaves. Lock gear, usually a simple valve or a pump, allows water to enter or leave the chamber. When a ship must maneuver through a steep incline in a waterway, several locks may be constructed close to each other in a series. At the Panama Canal, pumps are not needed to move the water. The flow of water at all locks is driven by gravity alone.

to secure. More rock was dumped into the river, and finally, the dam held. Ten days later, however, part of it broke loose. Workers took more than a week to repair it. But in the end, the semicircular-shaped dam held back the river, forcing the water behind to spread out and form a lake, the largest human-made one of its time.

The Gatun Dam was completed, the river was conquered, and Gatun Lake was created. Author Ian Cameron explained this important moment in his book *The Impossible Dream: The Building of the Panama Canal*, "The mighty river was finally transformed from a demon of destruction to a beast of burden, its waters no longer threatening the canal but harnessed to serve it."[2]

Sibert saw even greater potential in the river and decided to create a hydroelectric plant next to the dam. The force of the water powered giant turbine engines. One day, they would generate enough electricity to power the Panama Canal and the entire Canal Zone.

Mushy Soil

At the other end of the isthmus, Sydney B. Williamson led the team working on the Pacific

The Miraflores Locks

The two Miraflores locks are the first locks that ships encounter when entering the Panama Canal from the Pacific Ocean. After the Miraflores locks, ships proceed approximately .75 miles (1.2 km) across a small lake to a similar lock at Pedro Miguel. Electric mules, which are a type of powerful electric locomotive, move along the sides of the locks on rails. With steel wires, the mules steer the ship through the lock. Normally, a large ship requires six mules to transit the lock. Once ships pass through the Miraflores and Pedro Miguel locks, they are at the level of Gatun Lake, 85 feet (25.9 m) above sea level.

Division. Construction on that side of the canal was not without problems, either. The soil near the shore was like mush. Rocks that were dumped in one area merely caused another area to heave. Years of trying to strengthen the soil had proved unsuccessful. Goethals eventually stopped work near the shore and moved the project inland, to a site called Miraflores. Construction of a series of dams and locks at Miraflores went smoothly, and the Pacific team finished the locks in May 1913. But work in the Central Division was more problematic, and the Culebra Cut proved to be the biggest challenge of all.

*A recent view of Gatun Dam, including the
hydroelectric plant and spillway*

Canal workers stood atop train wreckage after a landslide in the Culebra Cut in 1913.

HELL'S GORGE

Major David Gaillard was in charge of the Central Division of the Panama Canal. The middle section—the longest at about 35 miles (56 km)—was called Hell's Gorge. Cutting through 9 miles (14.5 km) of the gorge, the Culebra Cut would be one of the greatest engineering feats of all time. Gaillard and his crew of 6,000 men would blast away 9 miles (14.5 km) of the Continental Divide and lower it to 40 feet (12 m) above sea level.

Every day, the men drilled holes in the mountainside and carefully placed explosives inside them. They detonated the explosives daily at noon and twilight. The times were set so everyone knew when to stay clear of the blasts. Steam shovels constantly scooped up soil and dumped it into railroad cars. The trains, approximately 160 daily, hauled away soil and rock 24 hours a day.

ENEMIES OF HELL'S GORGE

The work in the gorge had two enemies: heavy rainfall and landslides. Both were common, and cleanup after either one was massive. Rain fell between 250 and 270 days a year. After a torrential downpour on October 2, 1907, dirt and rock plummeted into Culebra Cut. The landslide overturned and nearly

David Du Bose Gaillard

David Du Bose Gaillard, head of construction at the Culebra Cut, suffered what seemed to be a nervous breakdown the summer after work at the Culebra Cut was completed. Gaillard returned to the United States, where doctors found a tumor on his brain. After surgery and treatment, Gaillard died in Baltimore, Maryland, on December 5, 1913, at the age of 54. The Culebra Cut was renamed the Gaillard Cut on April 27, 1915, in his memory.

buried two steam shovels. It also buried countless workers. For many, Culebra Cut became their grave. The slide also demolished railroad tracks, water pipes, and drainage systems. And the earth did not stop sliding. For the next ten days, the ground moved about 14 feet (4.3 m) a day. The men worked around the clock to rescue lives and salvage equipment.

There were numerous other landslides as well. As one worker from the West Indies put it, "Today you dig and tomorrow it slides."[1] An old Spanish worker said the ground was taking revenge against people who were trying to "dissect nature's creation."[2]

Despite the setbacks and catastrophes, the Culebra Cut was taking shape. It was a little deeper and a bit wider every day. Thousands of tourists came to gaze into the gorge and marvel at the "special wonder of the canal."[3] A U.S. traveler described the spectacular scene:

Panama's Climate

Panama has a tropical climate with a rainy season from April to December. Humidity is approximately 80 percent all year round, and average annual rainfall varies from 70 to 130 inches (178 to 330 cm) over different areas of the country. Much of that rainfall flows into Gatun Lake, keeping a constant source of water for the canal. Average temperatures range from 70 to 90 degrees Fahrenheit (21 to 32°C).

He who did not see the Culebra Cut during the mighty work of the excavation missed one of the great spectacles of all ages. . . . From its crest on a working day you looked down upon a mighty rift in the earth's crust, at the base of which pygmy engines and ant-like forms were rushing to and fro without seeming plan or reason. Through the murky atmosphere strange sounds rose up and smote the ear of the onlooker with resounding clamor. . . . Collectively the sounds were harsh, deafening, brutal such as we might fancy would arise from hell were the lid of that place of fire and torment to be lifted.[4]

Journalists tried to explain what it was like in the Culebra Cut in their articles. So much dirt was being removed, they said, that a train of cars carrying all of it would circle Earth four times at the equator.

Humans against Nature

With the tremendous work being done in the Culebra Cut, visitors marveled at the magnitude of project. Every day, the battle between humankind and nature raged on. There was a certain allure that both frustrated and nourished the spirit. One person observed:

No one could say when the sun went down what the condition of the [Culebra] Cut would be when the sun arose the next morning. The work of months and years might be blotted out by an avalanche of earth or the toppling over of a mountain of rock. It was a task to try men's souls, and it was also one to kindle in them a joy of combat which no repulse could chill, and a buoyant faith of ultimate victory which nothing could shake.[5]

A cargo ship amid the lush landscape of the Panama Canal

The Final Blast

At the end of September 1913, the work on the Culebra Cut was finished. All steam shovels, trains,

rails, drills, and dynamite were removed. Workers
left the area. Now it was time for the Culebra Cut
to be filled with water. During construction, the
floodwaters of the Chagres River had been held
back with a huge human-made dike. The earthen
dike now had to be blown away—and the president
of the United States was the best person to perform
this monumental act. Since March 1909, Woodrow
Wilson had been the U.S. president. The button to
detonate the explosives was installed on President
Wilson's desk in Washington DC. It was rigged to
relay a telegraph signal from Washington to New
York and then to Galveston, Texas, and on to
Panama. The signal would set off an explosion in
the center of the dike, opening up a gaping hole
to release the water. At 2:00 p.m. on October 10,
1913, Wilson pushed the button.

In Panama, there was a low rumble, followed
by a tremendous *boom!* Dirt from the dike spurted
into the sky. Then came a thunderous roar of water
pouring into the gorge. Some people cheered; others
cried. But then the water stopped. Dirt and rock had
blocked it about halfway through the Culebra Cut,
at a section called Cucaracha. For a week, workers
scrambled to blast away the obstruction, but nothing

The Workers Honored

In 1906, President Roosevelt authorized a medal to be given to U.S. citizens who worked on the Panama Canal. The size of a silver dollar, the medal was made of bronze, copper, and tin taken from machinery abandoned by the French. The worker's name and his years of service were engraved on the medal.

worked. Dynamite sent soggy soil and silt into the sky, but the dirt seemed to fall right back into the same hole. Then, on October 24, nature took over. It rained continuously for eight hours. The Chagres River flooded, and the level of Gatun Lake rose. At Cucaracha, the men dug a small trench at the top of the obstruction. At last, a tiny stream of water began to trickle past it. The trickle grew to a torrent with a force powerful enough to send water over the obstruction and fill the Culebra Cut.

The next morning, a sheet of beautiful blue water stretched across the entire Isthmus of Panama. It meandered through the lush jungle and between the tall mountains in a continuous path from the Atlantic Ocean to the Pacific. The Panama Canal was now filled with water. The two oceans were linked, and the world highway was nearly ready to serve all nations.

A cruise ship at Miraflores Locks in 2008

Onlookers watched as tugboat Gatun *made a successful trial run through the Gatun Locks on September 26, 1913.*

LAND DIVIDED, WORLD UNITED

A telegram from Washington DC arrived in Panama on August 15, 1914. Directed to Chief Engineer George Washington Goethals, it read, "A stupendous undertaking has been finally accomplished, and a perpetual memorial to the genius and enterprise of our people has been created."[1]

At 9:00 a.m., the SS *Ancon* began a historic voyage from the Atlantic Ocean to the Pacific. On board were the U.S. secretary of war, the president of Panama, and several hundred others. The breathtaking trip took 9 hours and 40 minutes. It was the culmination of 35 years of both French and U.S. construction and 400 years of dreams that divided a continent and united the world. Teddy Roosevelt never saw the completed canal, but he considered it his greatest achievement as president. Roosevelt died five years later, in 1919.

The Canal Is Finished and World War I Begins

Only a few observers silently waved flags on the banks, and no significant political figures were present for the historic event.

A Yearly Celebration

Every year, on August 14, a celebration commemorates the anniversary of the opening of the Panama Canal. A small boat with about 25 people on board journeys from the dock at the Pedro Miguel Lock, past huge ships, and through the Culebra Cut. Between the two highest mountains, where the sides of the canal are nearly vertical, the boat stops. The people toss flowers onto the water, say prayers, and sing hymns to remember the workers and the building of the canal.

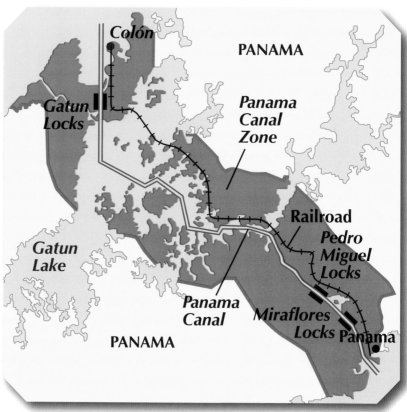

The Panama Canal Zone, 1903–1979

The *New York Times* published an article about the
opening of the Panama Canal—but it appeared on
page 14. The grandeur and triumph of the canal
had taken a backseat to another international event.
Germany had just declared war on France, and
countries all around the world were making alliances

and planning military strategies. This war would involve every continent and every ocean. It would come to be called World War I.

In the shadow of the war, the Panama Canal was still a success. Although commerce suffered during the war and ship traffic on the canal was sparse, the Panama Canal made a profit. Ships were charged a toll to transit the canal. Once the war ended in 1918, ships traveled more freely, and trade returned to normal.

On July 25, 1919, just a month after the official end of the war, a parade of 100 U.S. Navy ships entered the Panama Canal in a display of power and celebration. The parade had originally been set for August 15, 1914, but it had been postponed because of the war. Victorious but war-weary, the navy proudly showed off its fleet on a majestic voyage through the Panama Canal.

The Panama Canal has operated successfully now for nearly 100 years. Its history has not been without challenges and changes, however. Over the years, dirt continued to come loose and slide down the banks. In 1915, the canal closed for six months after a huge landslide. And in 1974, a slide reduced ship traffic, making it one way. But whenever necessary, canal workers put the dredges and steam shovels back to work and dug out the canal. As ships got bigger, the canal was cut wider and dredged deeper. More tugboats, towing locomotives, and floating equipment were purchased. However, the size of the locks cannot be changed, and in 2006 Nicaragua announced that it intended to build its own canal—one that will accommodate gigantic, modern ships.

Panama Takes Control of the Canal

The story of the Panama Canal has not been without controversy. Over the years, the Panamanians, as well as concerned people from other countries, have questioned U.S. control of the canal. The Canal Zone, necessary for building and operating the canal, became a thorn in Panama's side. The Panamanians displayed their resentment by rioting time and again—first in 1912, then in 1915, and then again in 1947, 1958, 1959, 1962, 1964, and 1968. Citizens from both Panama and the

Panama's Head of State General Omar Torrijos signs the Panama Canal Treaty in 1977. President Jimmy Carter, far left, looks on.

United States were killed in almost every riot. The 1964 riot was particularly violent, culminating on January 9 with the deaths of 21 Panamanians and 4 U.S. soldiers. In Panama, this day is now referred to as Martyrs' Day.

In 1977, President Jimmy Carter and others created a treaty that replaced the 1903 Hay-Bunau-Varilla Treaty. After a long debate, the Panama Canal Treaty, also known as the Torrijos-Carter Treaty, was ratified on September 7, 1977. Over a period of 20 years, the United States agreed to gradually turn over full control of the canal to Panama. However, the United States retained the right to defend the canal with military force if necessary.

On October 1, 1979, the United States completed the first phase of the treaty. It returned the 500-square-mile (1,295-sq-km) Canal Zone to Panama and phased out the U.S. government functions. On December 31, 1999, the formal transfer of the Panama Canal took place, and the Republic of Panama took full ownership and control of its operation.

Today, the Panama Canal remains one of the most important transoceanic routes in the world. It has improved commerce and travel for countless

An Expensive Trip

Each vessel that passes through the Panama Canal pays a toll. The toll is based on the vessel type, size, and cargo. The rate is different for passenger ships and ships carrying no cargo. In 1915, the canal took in approximately $4 million in tolls. By 1970, that figure exceeded $100 million. In 2008, revenue exceeded $2 billion.

In 2008, the 964-foot (294-m) cruise ship *Disney Magic* paid the highest toll on record—$331,200. The least expensive toll was 36 cents, paid by American Richard Halliburton, who swam the canal in 1928. For many cruise ships, crossing the Panama Canal is one of the main highlights for tourists. Most cruise ships pay large tolls, but they represent a small percentage of total transits. Cruise ships often compete with yachts and container vessels for space on the waterway. Slots to cross the canal are sometimes sold at auction to the highest bidder.

nations. Each year, an increased number of ships carry more tons of cargo through the canal. Ten years after the official opening, more than 5,000 ships were transiting the canal every year. By 1939, the number of ships topped 7,000, and today more than 15,000 ships transit the canal each year.

After nearly a century, the Panama Canal has passed the test of time. The seemingly impossible task begun by the French and completed by the United States fulfilled the dreams of many. And now the country where it resides—Panama—is successfully continuing the dream.

Panama not only maintains the canal but also continues to improve it. On September 3, 2007, in the sweltering heat and occasional rain, thousands of people gathered at Paraiso, just north of Panama City on the Pacific Ocean. Among them was Jimmy Carter, who had helped

Panama City

Panama City, located at the Pacific entrance of the Panama Canal, is the capital and largest city in Panama, with a population of more than 1 million. High-rise hotels, apartment buildings, and office complexes fill the skyline. According to *International Living* magazine, the city is one of the top five places for retirement in the world. It is also one of the fastest-growing cities in Latin America.

return the Canal Zone to Panama. As the people watched, an enormous blast took out a huge section of a hill. Thus work began on the $5.2 billion canal expansion project that will double the cargo capacity of the canal. The day before, a canal worker had been killed. The death served as a stark reminder of the tens of thousands of human lives that had already been lost in the construction of one of the finest achievements of all time. Other canals may be built, but none will take away the glory, the majesty, and the rich history of the Panama Canal.

An electric towing locomotive, called a "mule,"
helps steer ships through the canal locks.

TIMELINE

1502	1513	1534
Explorer Christopher Columbus lands at Portobelo on the north coast of Panama and explores the Chagres River.	Spanish conquistador Vasco Núñez de Balboa sees the Pacific Ocean off the coast of Panama.	King Charles V of Spain orders the clearing of the Chagres River and a survey of a path for a canal.

1881	1889	1901
France begins work on the Panama Canal, headed up by Ferdinand de Lesseps.	Lesseps abandons the Panama Canal project and retires in France.	Theodore Roosevelt becomes president of the United States.

1835	1849	1850
President Andrew Jackson sends U.S. Army engineers to Panama to determine the feasibility of building a canal.	Gold is discovered in California; gold prospectors seek a quicker route to the West.	American businessman William Aspinwall begins construction of the Panama Railroad.

1902	1903	1904
Congress votes in favor of a canal in Panama, not Nicaragua; the United States buys France's rights to a canal in Panama.	The United States approves the Hay-Herrán Treaty; Panamanians revolt against Colombia.	The United States begins work on the Panama Canal.

TIMELINE

1905–1906	1907	1910
Yellow fever reaches epidemic proportions, then is virtually eliminated in 1906.	The Panama Railroad is expanded across the Isthmus of Panama.	Gatun Dam is completed in the Atlantic Division, creating Gatun Lake.

1964	1974	1977
Panamanians riot against U.S. control of the Canal Zone, resulting in the deaths of 21 Panamanians and 4 U.S. soldiers.	A landslide in the Panama Canal reduces ship traffic to one way.	The United States ratifies the Panama Canal Treaty, which gradually turns over the Panama Canal to Panama.

1913

Work is finally completed on the Culebra Cut; the Panama Canal fills up with water.

1914

The Panama Canal officially opens; World War I begins.

1939

The number of ships transiting the Panama Canal each year tops 7,000.

1979

The Canal Zone is eliminated and becomes a part of Panama.

1999

Panama takes full ownership and control of the Panama Canal.

2007

Panama begins a $5.2-billion expansion project that will double the cargo capacity of the canal.

Essential Facts

Date of Event

1881 to August 15, 1914

Place of Event

Republic of Panama, Central America

Key Players

- ❖ Philippe Bunau-Varilla
- ❖ William Nelson Cromwell
- ❖ Ferdinand de Lesseps
- ❖ George Washington Goethals
- ❖ Dr. William Gorgas
- ❖ Theodore "Teddy" Roosevelt
- ❖ John Findley Wallace

Highlights of Event

❖ Spanish conquistador Vasco Núñez de Balboa traveled across the Isthmus of Panama in 1513 and saw the Pacific Ocean.

❖ The Gold Rush of 1849 heightened interest in a waterway between the oceans. The next year, construction of the Panama Railroad began.

❖ The French began work on a canal across Panama in 1881 but were forced to abandon the project in 1889.

❖ The United States enabled Panamanians to revolt against Colombian control in 1903 and declare Panama's independence.

❖ The United States began work on the canal in 1904; yellow fever was virtually eliminated in 1906.

❖ Gatun Dam was finished in 1910, creating the world's largest human-made lake of its time.

❖ The Panama Canal officially opened in 1914, the same year World War I broke out.

❖ The Canal Zone was eliminated and became a part of Panama in 1979.

❖ Panama took full ownership and control of the Panama Canal in 1999.

Quote

"No single great material work which remains to be undertaken on this continent is of such consequence to the American people."
—*Theodore "Teddy" Roosevelt*

ADDITIONAL RESOURCES

SELECT BIBLIOGRAPHY

Bullard, Arthur. *Panama: The Canal, the Country and the People*. Toronto: The MacMillan Co. of Canada, Ltd., 1914.

Cameron, Ian. *The Impossible Dream: The Building of the Panama Canal*. New York: William Morrow & Company, Inc., 1972.

Keller, Ulrich. *The Building of the Panama Canal in Historic Photographs*. New York: Dover Publications, 1983.

LaFeber, Walter. *The Panama Canal: The Crisis in Historical Perspective*. New York: Oxford University Press, 1989.

"Make the Dirt Fly!" *Smithsonian Institute Library*. 31 Dec. 2008 <http://www.sil.si.edu/Exhibitions/Make-the-Dirt-Fly/whybuild.html>

McCullough, David. *The Path Between the Seas*. New York: Simon and Schuster, 1977.

Parker, Matthew. *Panama Fever: The Epic Story of One of the Greatest Human Achievements of All Time—the Building of the Panama Canal*. New York: Doubleday, 2007.

FURTHER READING

Friar, William. *Portrait of the Panama Canal: From Construction to the Twenty-First Century*. Portland, OR: Graphic Arts Center Publishing Company, 2003.

Hassig, Susan M., and Lynette Quek. *Panama*. New York: Benchmark Books, 2007.

Ingram, Scott. *The Panama Canal*. San Diego, CA: Blackbirch Press, 2007.

Mann, Elizabeth. *The Panama Canal: The Story of How a Jungle Was Conquered and the World Made Smaller*. New York: Mikaya Press, 2006.

Web Links

To learn more about the building of the Panama Canal, visit
ABDO Publishing Company online at **www.abdopublishing.com**.
Web sites about the Panama Canal are featured on our Book Links
page. These links are routinely monitored and updated to provide
the most current information available.

Places to Visit

Miraflores Visitors Center
Panama Canal Authority, Miraflores Locks, Panama
507-276-8325
www.pancanal.com/eng/anuncios/cvm/index.html
This center offers sightseeing trips and displays exhibits about all
phases of construction and operation of the canal.

Panama Canal Museum
7985 113th Street, Suite 100, Seminole, FL 33772-4712
727-394-9338
www.panamacanalmuseum.org
This museum displays historic documents, photos, and items of the
Panama Canal era.

Panama Marine Adventures
Via Porras y Calle Belén, No. 106, Panama City, Panama
507-226-8917
www.pmatours.net
Experience a Panama Canal transit aboard the *Pacific Queen* (day
tours) and the *Discovery* (overnight expeditions).

GLOSSARY

ambassador
An official sent to another country as a representative of his or her own country.

avalanche
A fall or slide of a large mass, such as snow, rock, or a mountainside.

canal
An artificial waterway, often used for travel and shipping.

chloroform
A colorless, sweet-smelling liquid used at the Panama Canal site to kill mosquitoes.

commerce
The buying and selling of goods between cities or nations.

consul
A government representative who lives in a foreign country and acts on behalf of his or her own country's interests.

Continental Divide
A long stretch of high ground from which the rivers of a continent flow in opposite directions from each side.

coup
A successful takeover, usually of a government.

dynamite
A powerful explosive used in blasting or mining.

epidemic
A widespread outbreak of a contagious disease.

excavate
To remove by digging or scooping out.

fumigate
To use smoke or fumes in order to kill pests, such as mosquitoes.

hydroelectric
Run by electricity generated by the energy of running water.

insecticide
> A substance used to destroy insects.

isthmus
> A narrow piece of land that connects two larger masses of land.

lobby
> To attempt to influence public officials to take a certain action on legislation.

lock
> A closed-off section of a waterway in which vessels are raised or lowered by changing the water level in the section.

malaria
> An infectious disease transmitted to humans by the bite of an infected female *anopheles* mosquito and characterized by chills, fever, and sweating.

prospector
> A person who explores an area for minerals, such as gold, silver, or oil.

quarantine
> To isolate a person carrying a contagious disease in order to prevent the disease from spreading.

revolution
> The overthrow of a government by the people being governed.

sea level
> The level of the ocean's surface that is used as a standard in measuring land elevation or sea depth.

transit
> To pass across or through.

treaty
> A formal agreement between two or more states or nations.

yellow fever
> An infectious tropical disease transmitted by the *Aedes aegypti* mosquito. It causes fever and internal bleeding.

Source Notes

Chapter 1. "Make the Dirt Fly!"

1. "Smithsonian Tropical Research Institute: Fact Sheet." *Smithsonian Institution News*. April 2008. 16 Feb. 2009. <http://www.stri.org/english/about_stri/media/fact_sheet/STRI_factsheet_2008.pdf>.

2. Matthew Parker. *Panama Fever: The Epic Story of One of the Greatest Human Achievements of All Time—the Building of the Panama Canal*. New York: Doubleday, 2007. 292.

3. Ibid. 293.

4. Ibid.

5. Ibid.

6. Ibid. 295.

7. Ibid. 297.

8. Lydia M. Reid. "The Panama Canal Death Tolls." *The Silver People Heritage Foundation*. 17 Dec. 2008. 21 Jan. 2009 <http://thesilverpeopleheritage.wordpress.com/2008/12/17/the-panama-canal-death-tolls/>.

9. "Dr. William Gorgas and His War with the Mosquito." *Canadian Medical Association Journal*. 141 (1989): 599. Accessed at PubMed Central. National Institutes of Health. 31 Dec. 2008 <http://www.pubmedcentral.nih.gov/picrender.fcgi?artid=1451363&blobtype=pdf>.

10. Ibid.

Chapter 2. A Path Between the Seas

1. Matthew Parker. *Panama Fever: The Epic Story of One of the Greatest Human Achievements of All Time—the Building of the Panama Canal*. New York: Doubleday, 2007. 5.

2. Ibid. 6.

3. "To William Carmichael." 3 June 1788. *The Online Library of Liberty*. 13 Jan. 2009 <http://oll.libertyfund.org/?option=com_staticxt&staticfile=show.php%3Ftitle=802&chapter=86702&layout=html&Itemid=27>.

4. Matthew Parker. *Panama Fever: The Epic Story of One of the Greatest Human Achievements of All Time—the Building of the Panama Canal*. New York: Doubleday, 2007. 23.

5. "Make the Dirt Fly!" *Smithsonian Institute Library*. 31 Dec. 2008 <http://www.sil.si.edu/Exhibitions/Make-the-Dirt-Fly/whybuild.html>.

Chapter 3. The French Begin the Dig
1. David McCullough. *The Path Between the Seas*. New York: Simon and Schuster, 1977. 101.
2. Walter LaFeber. *The Panama Canal: The Crisis in Historical Perspective*. New York: Oxford University Press, 1989. 11.
3. Matthew Parker. *Panama Fever: The Epic Story of One of the Greatest Human Achievements of All Time—the Building of the Panama Canal*. New York: Doubleday, 2007. 111.
4. David McCullough. *The Path Between the Seas*. New York: Simon and Schuster, 1977. 89.
5. Matthew Parker. *Panama Fever: The Epic Story of One of the Greatest Human Achievements of All Time—the Building of the Panama Canal*. New York: Doubleday, 2007. 189.

Chapter 4. Nicaragua or Panama?
1. David McCullough. *The Path Between the Seas*. New York: Simon and Schuster, 1977. 280.
2. Ibid. 283.
3. Ibid. 287.
4. Tom Lansford. "Regime Formation and Maturation in the White House: The Rise of Internationalism During the Administration of Theodore Roosevelt." *White House Studies Compendium*. Ed. Robert W. Watson. Vol. 1. New York: Nova Science Publishers, 2007. 408.
5. Clay Jenkinson. "About Theodore Roosevelt (Biography)." *Theodore Roosevelt Center*. 16 Feb. 2009. <http://www.theodorerooseveltcenter.com/Kids/About_TR.asp>.

Source Notes Continued

Chapter 5. Roosevelt and Revolution

1. David McCullough. *The Path Between the Seas*. New York: Simon and Schuster, 1977. 351.
2. Ibid. 387.
3. Ibid. 386.
4. Ian Cameron. *The Impossible Dream: The Building of the Panama Canal*. New York: William Morrow & Company, Inc., 1972. 105.
5. Matthew Parker. *Panama Fever*. New York: Doubleday, 2007. 250-251.
6. Ibid. 251.
7. Ibid.
8. Ibid. 253.

Chapter 6. Jungle and Chaos

1. Ian Cameron. *The Impossible Dream: The Building of the Panama Canal*. New York: William Morrow & Company, Inc., 1972. 116.
2. Ibid. 105.
3. Matthew Parker. *Panama Fever*. New York: Doubleday, 2007. 255.
4. Ibid. 259.
5. Ian Cameron. *The Impossible Dream: The Building of the Panama Canal*. New York: William Morrow & Company, Inc., 1972. 122.
6. Ibid 123.
7. "Taft's Bitter Words: Official Statement About Sunday's Meeting—Wallace Sought Place." *New York Times*, 30 June 1905. p. 1. 16 Feb. 2009, <http://query.nytimes.com/gst/abstract.html?res=9 404E2DA173DE733A25753C3A9609C946497D6CF>.

Chapter 7. Preparing to Dig

1. David McCullough. *The Path Between the Seas*. New York: Simon and Schuster, 1977. 462.
2. Ibid. 617.
3. Matthew Parker. *Panama Fever*. New York: Doubleday, 2007. 407.
4. Ian Cameron. *The Impossible Dream: The Building of the Panama Canal*. New York: William Morrow & Company, Inc., 1972. 153.
5. Ibid. 165.
6. Ibid. 167.

Chapter 8. Building the Locks

1. Matthew Parker. *Panama Fever*. New York: Doubleday, 2007. 398.
2. Ian Cameron. *The Impossible Dream: The Building of the Panama Canal*.
New York: William Morrow & Company, Inc., 1972. 193.

Chapter 9. Hell's Gorge

1. Matthew Parker. *Panama Fever*. New York: Doubleday, 2007. 422.
2. Ibid.
3. Ulrich Keller. *The Building of the Panama Canal in Historic Photographs*.
New York: Dover Publications, Inc., 1983. viii.
4. Matthew Parker. *Panama Fever*. New York: Doubleday, 2007. 422.
5. David McCullough. *The Path Between the Seas*. New York. Simon and
Schuster, 1977.

Chapter 10. Land Divided, World United

1. Ulrich Keller. *The Building of the Panama Canal in Historic Photographs*.
New York: Dover Publications, Inc., 1983. 106.
2. Robert H. Sprague. "Panama Canal Zone—Historical Flag."
7 Jan. 1999. *U.S. Governor of the Panama Canal Zone: Flags of the World*. 16
Feb. 2009. <http://www.crwflags.com/fotw/flags/pa-cz.html>.

INDEX

ABOUT THE AUTHOR

Sue Vander Hook has been writing and editing books for more than 15 years. Although her writing career began with several nonfiction books for adults, her main focus is educational books for children and young adults. She especially enjoys writing about historical events and biographies of people who made a difference. Her published works also include a high school curriculum and several series on disease, technology, and sports. Vander Hook lives with her family in Minnesota.

PHOTO CREDITS

Library of Congress, cover, 6, 11, 55, 60, 70, 86; North Wind Picture Archives, 9, 18, 27, 28, 32, 37, 46, 96, 97 (top), 97 (bottom), 98 (top); Hulton Archive/Getty Images, 17; Maps.com/ Corbis, 38; AP Images, 45, 51, 69, 78, 91, 98 (bottom), 99 (top); Corbis, 52; National Archives/Corbis, 59; Bettmann/Corbis, 66; Red Line Editorial, 72, 88; Tomas Van Hourtryve/AP Images, 77; Danny Lehman/Corbis, 82; Nevada Wier/Getty Images, 85, 99 (bottom); Andres Balcazar/iStockphoto, 95